FUNtastic FROGS

Air

By Jill Osofsky

Published by Ideal School Supply
an imprint of

McGraw-Hill Children's Publishing

Air • Grades K-2

Special thanks to my parents, Fred and Jeannette Evely, who always encouraged my scientific curiosity and tolerated all the creatures I brought home. Especially the snake that got loose in the garage!

McGraw-Hill Children's Publishing
A Division of The McGraw·Hill Companies

Published by Ideal School Supply
An imprint of McGraw-Hill Children's Publishing
Copyright ©2001 McGraw-Hill Children's Publishing

Cover Concept and Page Design: Sara Mordecai
Cover Art: Warner McGee
Text Illustrations: Sherry Neidigh

Limited Reproduction Permission: Permission to duplicate these materials is limited to the person for whom they are purchased. Reproduction for an entire school or school district is unlawful and strictly prohibited.

Send all inquiries to:
McGraw-Hill Children's Publishing
3195 Wilson Drive NW
Grand Rapids, MI 49544

All Rights Reserved • Printed in the United States of America.

Funtastic Frogs™: Air, Grades K–2
ISBN: 1-56451-377-7

2 3 4 5 6 7 8 9   05 04 03 02 01

Table of Contents

Notes to the Teacher 4
Guidelines for Science Safety 7
It's Everywhere (air) 8
Now You See It (air in water) 10
Light as Air? (air has weight) 12
The Air Down There (air occupies space) 14
Getting Warmer (warm air expands) 16
Rise and Shine (warm air rises) 18
Air Power (force) 20
Air Lift (compressed air) 22
What Pressure! (air pressure) 24
Make a Frog-copter (air resistance) 26
Take Flight (air and flight) 28
A Fabulous Flyer (air and flight) 30
Glossary 32

Notes to the Teacher

Children are natural scientists. They are innately curious and constantly wonder why. They ask questions, make predictions, and describe observations about everything from the stars in the sky to the slugs in the garden. Children thrive on being actively involved in learning, using their hands and their minds to seek answers to questions about their world.

This book is written for those young scientists and their teachers. It is one in a series of books designed to encourage children's inquiry into physical science. It is designed to make learning and teaching about science fun and easy.

As children do the activities in this book, they will actively explore the properties of air and how those properties affect our daily life. Some activities require the use of Funtastic Frog™ Counters. Funtastic Frog™ Counters can be purchased from Ideal School Supply or your Ideal School Supply dealer. Please visit our Web site at: *www.MHteachers.com*.

Each activity in this book is designed for hands-on, minds-on science inquiry. Each investigation has been written to be safe, developmentally appropriate, and done with common materials and minimal preparation. The activities support current National Science Education Standards.

The science process skills developed in this book include:
- observing and asking questions about everyday events
- describing properties
- classifying objects
- predicting outcomes
- talking about and describing results

Contents
This book contains 12 activities. A teacher page precedes each student activity page. Each teacher page gives an overview of the activity as well as the science background you will need to make connections between the activities. The science process skills, materials needed, suggestions for grouping the children, and the procedure for the activity are included on the teacher page. The student page is used for recording.

Suggestions for Classroom Use
The activities in this book can be done as a whole class, in small groups, or set up at a learning center. You may choose to introduce the activities to the whole group and have them completed in small groups or individually.

Try each activity before presenting it to the class to familiarize yourself with the procedure and possible management issues. You may wish to make an overhead transparency of the student page to facilitate student recording. Consider asking parents or older children to volunteer to act as lab assistants during the activities. Organize the materials for each group in plastic tubs or on trays for easy distribution.

To integrate literacy with your science activities, use a word wall to reference key concepts, word meanings, and spelling. Choose a large area for a word wall display. Place chart paper boxes or "bricks" in the area. When new science words are introduced, write the word on a brick and place it on the word wall. Use the bricks to review word meanings and concepts. Hold the children responsible for correct spelling and use of the words on the wall. Incorporate writing activities to use and review the words.

When discussing predictions with children emphasize that it is okay if their predictions are not "right!" Making predictions is a very important part of the scientific process. Real scientists often make predictions that are not correct. When that happens, they keep trying until they find the answer to the question they are investigating.

Plan to allow adequate time for discussion after each activity. Talking about their discoveries helps children make connections to daily experiences. Class discussions encourage the type of thinking required for further inquiry and problem solving.

Above all, relax and have fun with these activities! Attitudes toward science are formed during these early years. You can be a positive role model who encourages the development of scientific inquiry and literacy in our ever-changing world.

Introducing the Activities

If the children are new to the Funtastic Frog™ Counters, allow time for the children to freely explore the counters. This will satisfy their curiosity about the frogs before using them in the activities. Talk about the properties of the frogs such as color, texture, size, and weight. Encourage children to compare, sort, and classify the frogs and describe their reasoning. Discuss whether the frogs are alive or not alive and why.

Read and discuss the key question for each activity. Show the materials and how they will be used. Define and discuss new words. Invite children to predict what will happen, then pass out the activity sheet. Model new techniques to be sure children clearly understand the task before they work in small groups or independently.

Each of the activities uses science process skills. You can provide practice in identifying and using these processes by pointing them out as you use them with the class. In discussions ask questions that encourage the children to use these processes. Ask questions such as:

What do you think will happen?

How could we find out about _____?

What do you see or hear?

What might happen if you tried this?

How are these alike or different?

What do you think these results mean?

What else can we try?

Guidelines for Science Safety

Safety is an important aspect of any science program. The activities in this book have been carefully developed with safety in mind and present no safety hazards for children when used with appropriate supervision and reasonable care. However, before starting any activity, it is always good to review the dos and don'ts of handling the materials. When necessary, specific safety tips are included.

The safety guidelines listed here are based on those recommended by the National Science Teachers Association. Though it is a partial list, we urge you and your children to use it to help create a safe classroom atmosphere for scientific exploration.

Obtain a copy of your state and local regulations that relate to school safety, as well as a copy of your school district's policies and procedures for accidents and safety.

Check your classroom on a regular basis to ensure that all possible safety precautions are being taken. Equipment and materials should be properly stored. Spills should be wiped up immediately.

At the start of each science activity, remind children of relevant safety procedures. Caution them about the use of plastic bags, sharp objects, and any fragile glassware. When the children experiment with air pressure and flying objects be sure to use a space that allows plenty of room between groups.

Have the children report any accident or injury to you immediately, no matter how minor.

Stress that children must never touch or taste any substance unless they have received specific instructions from you to do so.

For more details on science and safety, an excellent reference entitled *Safety in the Elementary Science Classroom* may be ordered from:
National Science Teachers Association
1840 Wilson Boulevard
Arlington, VA 22201-3000
Voice: (800) 243-7100
Web site: *www.nsta.org*

It's Everywhere!

Overview
The activities in this book demonstrate how fascinating simple concepts can be when you investigate them closely. The concept that air is everywhere sounds simple, but it will be fascinating for the children in your class to discover. Remind the children about safe use of plastic bags in this activity. The bag should not be placed on the face or over the head of any child.

Science Process Skills: Observing, recording, reporting

Materials for each child:
• a plastic bag

Procedure
1. Access prior knowledge by asking the children to tell you what they know about air. Record their statements on the chalkboard or on a chart for reference.

2. Collect air in a plastic bag by pulling it through the air. Twist the end of the bag to contain the air. Ask the children to tell you what is inside. They will probably answer *air*. Explain that an ocean of air surrounds us on earth. Encourage them to move their arms in a swimming motion to feel the air around them.

3. Distribute the plastic bags and allow the children to capture some air.

4. Encourage the children to describe how they captured air. Ask questions such as, *Where is air?* (almost everywhere around us but not in space) *Can we see air?* (not usually, but we can see something filled with air, like a balloon) *Can we feel air?* (yes, when we move through air or when air is moving around us, as on a windy day)

Making Connections
Encourage the children to discuss the ways animals and people use air.

ACTIVITY 1

Name_____

It's Everywhere!

Draw what you did to collect some air.

Draw one way a person or animal uses air.

Now You See It

Overview
This activity allows children to observe the air in water. While cold water keeps the air in water dissolved, the children should be able to observe the tiny air bubbles on the frog and the sides of the cup in the warmed water.

Science Process Skills: Predicting, observing, recording, communicating

Materials for each pair or group of children:
- a large frog
- a clear plastic cup
- cold tap water

Procedure

1. Invite the children to describe what is in the empty cup. (Some children may recall that it is filled with air, others will say it is empty.)

2. Ask them to predict if they think there is air in water. Have them record their predictions on the activity sheet.

3. Model to show how full to fill the cup. Have the children use cold tap water to fill their cups. Encourage them to look through the side of the cup and describe what they see.

4. Next, tell them to place the large frog inside the cup of water, then set the glass in a warm place to observe. Within a few minutes they should see tiny air bubbles on the frog and the on the sides of the cup.

5. Discuss their observations, comparing them to their predictions. Point out that the air bubbles they observed were dissolved in the cold water. As the water warmed up, the dissolved air gathered together in the tiny bubbles.

Making Connections
Talk about what group of animals uses the air in water to breathe. You might bring in some goldfish to the classroom for the children to observe. Inexpensive feeder fish are available at most tropical fish stores.

Now You See It

Question: Does water contain air?

Circle your guess.

Yes, water does contain air.   No, there is no air in water.

1. Use cold water to fill the cup 2/3 full. Draw what you see in the cup.
2. Place the frog in the bottom of the cup.
3. Place the cup in a warm place to observe.
4. Draw what you see in the cup of warm water.

WHAT DID YOU FIND OUT?

Light as Air?

Overview
Placing a pair of balloons on a balance allows the children to see that air has mass (weight). Latex balloons, such as those sold in party stores, are easy to inflate and work well in this activity. If your balance has buckets, it will be easier to complete this demonstration if you insert the balloon in the bucket then inflate it. This will hold the balloon in place inside the bucket without popping it.

Note: While *mass* is the correct term to describe the amount of matter in the balloon, for this age level it is acceptable to use the term *weight*.

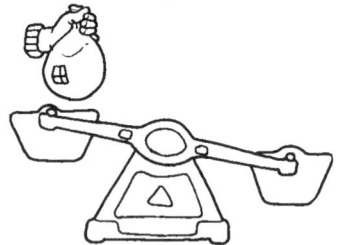

Science Process Skills: Observing, predicting, recording

Materials for a class demonstration:
- two same-sized balloons
- a balance

Procedure
1. Invite the class to relate what they already know about air. Ask them to predict whether air has weight. Have them record their predictions on the activity sheet.

2. Show two uninflated balloons. Invite one child to use the balance and verify that the balloons weigh the same.

3. Inflate one balloon. Ask what you used to take up the space inside the balloon. (air)

4. Have one child come up and compare the weights of the inflated and uninflated balloons. Repeat the comparison as many times as needed.

5. Discuss the results. Ask questions such as, *How were the balloons the same? What is different about the two balloons? What do you think is in the inflated balloon?* (air) *Does air have weight?* (Yes, the inflated balloon is heavier than the uninflated balloon.)

Extensions
Use small frogs or paper clips and the balance to measure the weight (mass) of the air in the balloon.

Allow the children to repeat the activity using different sizes of balloons.

Light as Air?

Question: Does air have weight?

Circle your guess.

Yes, air has weight.　　　　No, air has no weight.

Draw what you observed in the activity.

WHAT DID YOU FIND OUT?

The Air Down There

Overview
This activity demonstrates that even if you can't see it, air occupies space.

Science Process Skills: Observing, predicting, recording

Materials for a class demonstration:
- copy paper, tissue, or a paper towel
- a tall clear plastic cup
- an aquarium

Procedure

1. Show the children the materials. Invite two children to come up to assist you. One will crumple the paper and the other will push it into the cup so that it stays in place when inverted.

2. Ask the class what they think will happen if someone puts the cup in the water. Will the paper get wet? Have the children record their predictions on the activity sheet.

3. Have another child hold the cup upside-down and push it down into the water. Ask the class what they observe happening.

4. Carefully remove the inverted glass from the water. Have a fourth child come up to feel the paper when the cup comes out of the water.

5. Discuss. Ask questions such as, *What do you think stopped the water from going into the glass? Why is the paper still dry?* (The glass was full of air. The air took up space in the glass. There was no room for the water to come in to wet the paper.)

Extension
You can prove that air is inside the cup using this demonstration. Use a nail to poke a hole in the bottom of a paper or plastic cup. Holding your finger over the hole, push the inverted cup into the water. Remove your finger. Water will enter the cup, forcing the air out the hole in the cup. The children will be able to observe bubbles of air rising to the surface.

ACTIVITY 4

Name_____

The Air Down There

Question: Will paper in an upside-down glass get wet when it is pushed into water?

Circle your guess.

Yes, the paper will get wet.   No, the paper will stay dry.

Draw what you observe.

WHAT DID YOU FIND OUT?

Getting Warmer

Overview
This activity demonstrates that warm air expands.

Science Process Skills: Observing, predicting, recording

Materials for a class demonstration:
- a balloon (one that has been inflated then deflated)
- a plastic bottle with a narrow neck
- a pan or bowl large enough to hold the bottle
- hot water

Procedure

1. Ask the children to tell you what is in the bottle. (air) Then ask them to predict will happen when you heat the air in the bottle. Discuss their ideas, then have them record their predictions on the activity sheet.

2. Model how to place the balloon over the mouth of the bottle, letting it hang limply on the side.

3. Put the bottle in the bowl, then fill it with hot water. Have the children observe closely.

4. Discuss. Ask questions such as, *What was in the bottle before the balloon was put on it?* (air) *What happened when the bottle was placed in the water?* (The air inside the bottle was heated.) *What made the balloon inflate?* (The heated air expanded, filling up the balloon.)

Extension
Have the children predict what will happen as the air inside the bottle cools. (The balloon will deflate.)

Getting Warmer

Question: What happens when air is heated?

Circle your guess.

Heated air will shrink.   Heated air will expand.

Draw what your observed.

WHAT DID YOU FIND OUT?

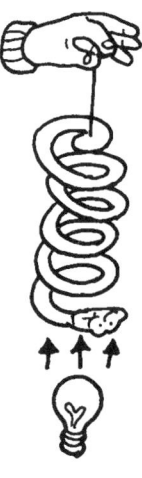

Rise and Shine

Overview
This activity demonstrates that warm air rises, causing movement.

Science Process Skills:
Predicting, observing, recording

Materials for each child:
- one copy of page 19
- scissors
- tape
- string or thread, about 24 inches long
- colored markers, pencils, or crayons
- a heat source (a light bulb)

Procedure

1. Talk with the children about what they know happens to air when it is heated. (it expands)

2. Ask the children to predict what else warm air might do. Discuss their ideas. Record their predictions on the chalkboard.

3. Distribute the activity sheet and have the children color the design.

4. Point out the cutting lines on the design, then have the children cut out their spiral. Distribute the string and tape as the children are cutting out the shape. Show them how and where to attach the string.

5. Assign different groups to visit the heat source, holding their spiral above the heat and observing what happens.

6. Discuss the results with the class. Ask questions such as, *What happens when the spiral is held above the light? Why do you think the spiral begins to turn? How does the air above the light bulb feel? What does the warm air do?* Guide the discussion to help the children observe that the light bulb heats the air above it, causing the air to rise. The heated air flows along the spiral, causing it to turn.

Making Connections
Take a walk outdoors on a warm day to let the children see the warm air rising off the surface of the heated playground surface.

Heated air above the surface of the ground allows birds of prey to seemingly coast in the air. The birds are actually riding warm air currents called thermals. If your school is located near where vultures or hawks fly, take the class out to observe their flight. If you live in an urban area you might schedule a field trip to see the birds or bring in books about birds of prey.

Rise and Shine

Question: What does warm air do?

1. Color and cut out the frog design.
2. Tape a piece of string in the center top of the design.
3. Hold your spiral over a heat source.

Air Power

Overview
This activity introduces the relationship between air and force. Force is defined as a push or pull that moves objects. When the children blow on the frogs they push air from one space to another, causing movement.

Science Process Skills: Observing, comparing, experimenting, recording

Materials for each child:
- one small, one medium, and one large frog
- one straw

Procedure
1. Begin this investigation by distributing the frogs only. Challenge the children to find a way to move the frogs without touching them. Allow about five minutes for experimentation.

2. Discuss. Ask questions such as, *How did you move the frogs? Why did the frogs move?* Place special emphasis on examples using blown air.

3. Distribute the straws and invite the children to use air to move the frogs again. Ask questions such as, *Which way moved the frogs the farthest, blowing on them or using the straw to blow? Why might that be?* (The air in the straw directs a more concentrated movement of air than through the mouth.) *Which size frog moved the farthest?* (The size or mass of the frog can be a factor. Larger objects are harder to move.)

4. Discuss. Ask, *What did you discover about air in this activity?* (Air has a force that can push or move objects.)

Making Connections
Talk about the ways people use this property of air for pleasure or comfort. The children may mention sports that use air power such as sailboats or wind surfing. You might show pictures of windmills and wind-powered generators. Discuss how air makes them move. Invite the children to find other ways people use air power for work or pleasure.

Name_____

Air Power

Question: Can air move objects?

1. Line up one small, one medium, and one large frog.
2. Blow on each frog to move it.
3. Use the straw to blow on the frogs.
4. Compare. Which way moved the frogs farther?

WHAT DID YOU FIND OUT?

Air Lift

Overview
In this activity, the children observe that compressed air, such as in a balloon, creates a strong force (push) that can lift heavy objects.

Science Process Skills: Observing, predicting, experimenting, recording

Materials for a class demonstration:
- a large frog
- two or three books
- a balloon

Procedure
1. Place the frog on top of the book and ask the children how you could use the balloon to move the frog. They will probably suggest that you blow up the balloon then release the air, allowing it to push the frog off. Choose a child to try the suggested method or perform the experiment yourself.

2. Discuss the results, guiding the children to use the terms *air*, *push*, and *force*.

3. Ask the children to guess whether air and a balloon can lift a heavy book. Have them record their predictions. Ask the children to suggest a way to use air to lift the books.

4. Place the balloon near the edge of a table and place the heavy book on top of it.

5. Blow up the balloon while the book is on top of it.

6. Discuss. Ask, *What lifted the book?* (The push from air in the balloon.)

Extension
Invite children to invent a machine that lifts things using the push from air.

Air Lift

Question: Can air lift heavy objects?

Circle your guess.

Yes, air can lift heavy objects.   No, air cannot lift heavy objects.

Draw or write what you observed.

WHAT DID YOU FIND OUT?

What Pressure!

Overview
Air pressure affects the weather as well as the dynamics of flight. While the concept of air pressure is probably too sophisticated for this age child, the children will enjoy observing how air pressure affects common objects.

What may seem like magic is just the force of air pressing against the surface of each object. The air pressure under the card is stronger than gravity's pull on the water. As a result, the card remains in place.

Science Process Skills: Predicting, observing, and recording

Materials for a class demonstration:
- one plastic cup
- a card to cover the plastic cup
- a jug or pitcher of water
- a tub or bucket to catch spills

Procedure
1. Show the empty cup to the children and ask what they already have discovered about air so far. (Air is everywhere, it takes up space, air can move and lift things.)

2. Fill the cup to the brim with water. Tell the children that you are going to put the card on top of the cup, turn it upside-down, and remove your hand.

3. Ask the children what they think will happen. Have the children record their predictions, drawing what they think will happen to the water in the cup.

4. After all the predictions are made, turn the cup over while holding the card in place. Then remove your hand. (Air pressure will hold the card in place!)

5. Discuss. Ask questions such as, *What made you think the card would fall?* (Gravity pulls objects down toward the ground.) *What held the card in place?* (air pressure)

Extensions
Put plastic cups, cards, and liquids in a discovery area. Allow the children to try the same experiment using water and other liquids.

Squeezing an empty plastic catsup or mustard container will demonstrate the effect of air under pressure. The children can squeeze the bottle to blow air into water or direct the air flow at dominoes, index cards, or other objects to move them.

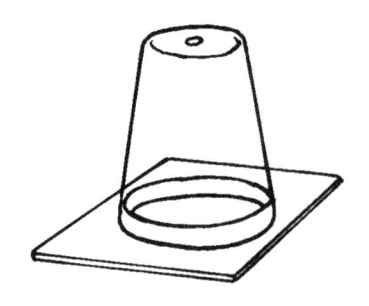

What Pressure!

Question: Will water always spill out of an upside-down cup?

Draw what you think will happen when the cup of water is turned upside down with the card on it.

Draw what you observed when the cup of water was turned upside down.

WHAT DID YOU FIND OUT?

Make a Frog-copter

Overview
Air resists the movement of an object traveling through it. This causes such objects as parachutes, gliders, and helicopters to fall more slowly. The helicopter model on page 27 will allow children to observe this firsthand.

Science Process Skills: Observing, predicting, experimenting, recording

Materials for each child:
- one small frog
- scissors
- tape

Procedure
1. Remind the children that in the last activity they learned that air pressure can be stronger than the pull of gravity. Encourage them to think of how they might be able to use air pressure to help keep something from falling. Prompt them to think of a parachute if needed.

2. Demonstrate the procedure for making the frog-copter:
- Cut on the solid lines.
- Fold as directed on the dotted lines.
- Tape the small frog on the bottom edge. (The weight of the frog helps the frog-copter perform better.)

3. Ask for suggestions for testing the frog-copter. Children will quickly come up with several ideas for testing. You may wish to allow the children to stand on a play structure outside to test their frog-copters.

4. Discuss. Ask questions such as, *Why didn't the helicopter just fall to the ground?* (Air resists the movement of the "rotors" on the frog-copter. Air resists the pull of gravity.)

Extensions and Connections
The children can experiment using different materials to investigate how that affects the movement of the helicopter. They might also experiment using different sizes and shapes for the rotors. Ask, *What happens if you use a large frog? No frog?*

The first helicopter came from nature. Take the children on a walk to look for seeds, such as those on maple trees, that travel in the same way as the helicopter the children made. Look for other examples in nature where air resists the movement of objects falling through it. (Leaves, dandelion seeds, and feathers are a few examples.)

Name_____

Make a Frog-copter!

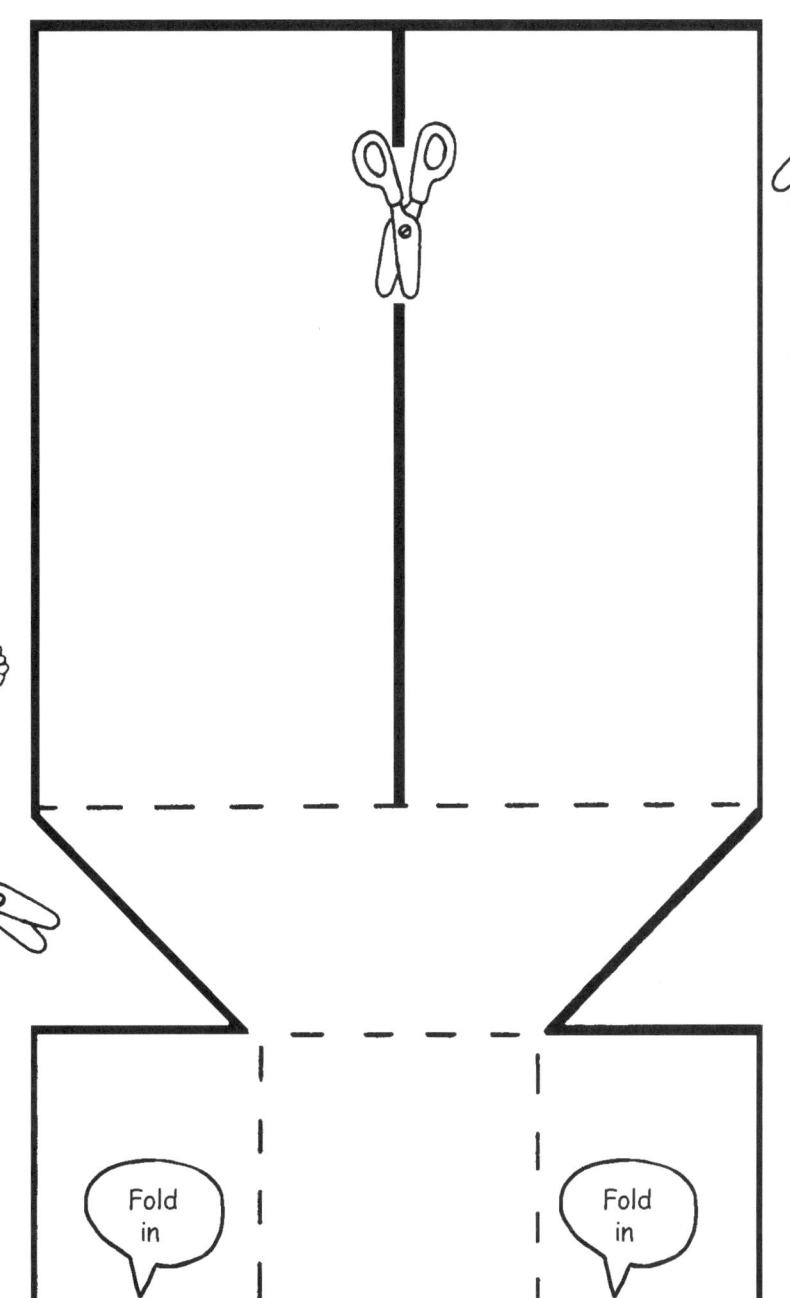

ACTIVITY 10

Cut on solid lines

Fold forward

Fold back

Fold in

Fold in

© McGraw-Hill Children's Publishing • ID43204 *Funtastic Frogs™: Air*

Take Flight

Overview

This demonstration will give children an idea of how the wings of an airplane help lift it off the ground. The demonstration is most successful when the children hold the wing close to the surface of their desk or table. When they blow over the top surface of the paper wing, it lowers the air pressure above the wing. The higher air pressure under the wing creates a lift effect.

The faster air moves, the less pressure it has. The top surface of a wing is curved, causing air to move faster over the top of the wing than under it. This creates lower air pressure above the wing. The slower-moving air under the wing has more pressure, causing the lift effect. As the speed of an airplane increases, the lift effect increases.

Science Process Skills: Observing, predicting, recording

Materials for each child:
- a 4 x 10-inch piece of paper
- tape
- a pencil

Procedure

1. Encourage the children to think about how air helps keep planes in flight. Tell the children that they are going to make a model of an airplane wing to discover how air can lift a plane.

2. Have the children tape the short ends of the paper together, and then place a pencil through the folded end of the wing.

3. Next have them predict what will happen when they blow under the wing. After they have recorded their predictions let them try it.

4. Discuss. The wing will rattle and vibrate, but it won't lift. The air moving faster below the wing has less pressure than above the wing. The heavier air pressure above the wing presses it down.

5. Have them predict what will happen when they blow over the top surface of the wing. Have them record their predictions then try it.

6. Discuss. The taped end of the wing should lift. The fast-moving air above the wing has less pressure than the air below the wing. The air pressure below the wing lifts the end of the wing.

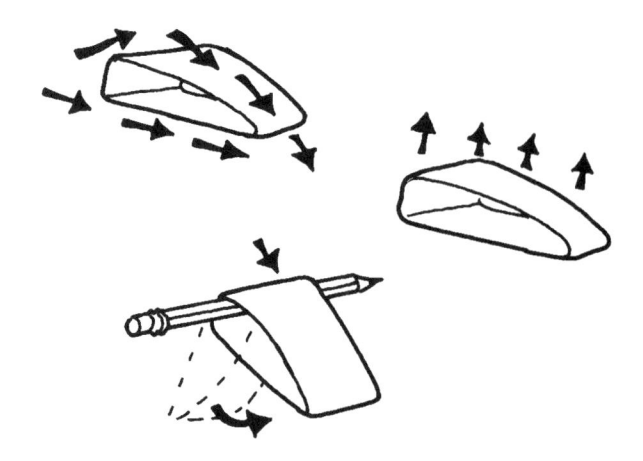

Name_____

Take Flight

Question: What causes an airplane wing to lift?

1. Tape the short ends of the paper strip together.
2. Place a pencil in the large open end of the wing.

3. Circle your guess. What will happen when you blow under the wing?

   The wing will lift up.   The wing will not lift up.

4. Try it. Record what happens.

5. Circle your guess. What will happen when you blow over the top of the wing?

   The wing will lift up.   The wing will not lift up.

6. Try it. Record what happens.

WHAT DID YOU FIND OUT?

A Fabulous Flyer

Overview
Children will enjoy using all they know about air, air pressure, speed, and flight in this activity. The design of the wing helps create the needed lift. The dynamics of speed and air pressure will determine how long the flyer remains aloft.

To launch the flyer, hold it between the two peaks and gently toss or push it forward.

Science Process Skills: Observing, experimenting

Materials for each child:
- a piece of 8 1/2 x 11-inch paper
- tape

Procedure
1. Fold the paper on the diagonal. This will create an unsymmetrical top with two peaks.

2. Fold up the bottom edge about 1/2-inch. Do this two times.

3. Slide the two ends together and tape.

4. Hold the flyer as shown, then gently toss it.

Extensions
Integrate math with this activity. Have the children take turns launching their flyers, then compare and measure the distances flown using standard or nonstandard units of measure.

Let the children experiment with the design, creating their own flyers.

Have a flight day. Allow children to bring in other examples of paper flyers. Measure and compare the distances covered by different designs.

Name_____

A Fabulous Flyer

1. Fold the paper on the diagonal. This will make two peaks.

2. Fold up the bottom edge about 1/2-inch. Do this two times.

3. Slide the two ends together and tape.

4. Hold your flyer between the two peaks, then toss it.

Glossary

aerodynamics – the study of the forces that act on objects moving through air

air – an invisible mixture of gases that make up our atmosphere

air pressure – the force of air per square inch

force – a push or pull that causes movement

mass – the amount of matter in an object

weight – the force of gravity upon an object